inspiration and
motivation for
RUNNERS

Ali Clarke

summersdale

INSPIRATION AND MOTIVATION FOR RUNNERS

Summersdale Publishers Ltd
46 West Street
Chichester
West Sussex
PO19 1RP
UK

www.summersdale.com

Printed and bound in the Czech Republic

ISBN: 978-1-84953-705-6

Substantial discounts on bulk quantities of Summersdale books are available to corporations, professional associations and other organisations. For details contact Nicky Douglas by telephone: +44 (0) 1243 756902, fax: +44 (0) 1243 786300 or email: nicky@ summersdale.com.

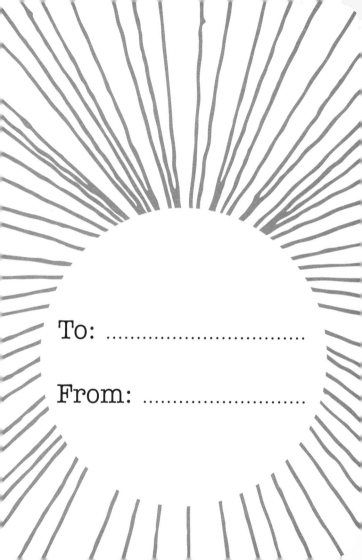

To: ....

From: ....

I RUN BEST

WHEN I RUN FREE.

STEVE PREFONTAINE

Every day is a good day when you run.

The difference
between the
impossible
and the
possible
lies in a person's
determination.

TOMMY LASORDA

Warming up too intensely before a run can detract from your efforts during the run itself. Instead of a sequence of deep stretches, try warming up with a 3–5-minute gentle walk, followed by a 5-minute run–walk.

MY OUTLOOK IS THAT
I NEVER WANT TO LOOK
BACK AND WONDER HOW
FAST I COULD HAVE BEEN.

DOUG MOCK

If you're starting out as a runner, avoid taking on too much at the beginning. If you haven't done much exercise recently you are more likely to have a low injury threshold. Instead of running too far, too quickly and too frequently, build up your stamina, pace and distance gradually. Some people like to do this using the 10 per cent rule – adding no more than 10 per cent to the distance of your run per week.

A JOURNEY OF A
THOUSAND MILES BEGINS
WITH A SINGLE STEP.

LAO TZU

Sleep longer.
Eat better.
Run faster.
Aim higher.
Be happier.

If there's any activity
happier,
more exhilarating,
more nourishing to the
imagination,
I can't think what
it might be.

JOYCE CAROL OATES ON RUNNING

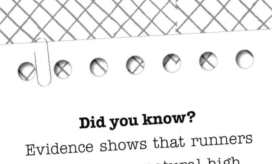

Did you know?

Evidence shows that runners
experience a natural high
when they go out for a run.
This is due to the release of
feel-good hormones called
endocannabinoids. Running
is also good therapy for
anxiety and depression.

I'LL BE HAPPY IF RUNNING AND I CAN GROW OLD TOGETHER.

HARUKI MURAKAMI

If you lack motivation, joining a running club could encourage you to run more regularly. As well as giving you the opportunity to socialise with people who share a similar interest, there are a number of other benefits that might suit your motivational needs. For example, you can enter races with your fellow club runners who can offer great support and guidance, you'll receive advice and tips from more experienced runners and be able to go to club-run social nights.

THE REASON WE RACE ISN'T SO
MUCH TO BEAT EACH OTHER...
BUT TO BE *WITH* EACH OTHER.

CHRISTOPHER MCDOUGALL

Running is life with the volume turned up.

Running **cleared** the day's cobwebs from my **mind** and focused my **thinking.**

JEFF HOROWITZ

Make sure you hydrate
yourself throughout the day
before you run; this will
make you feel more energised
and your body supple.

THERE IS NO TIME TO THINK
ABOUT HOW MUCH I HURT;
THERE IS ONLY TIME TO RUN.

BEN LOGSDON

Running myths debunked

'You can only improve by running every day' – studies say that you should run 3–4 times a week for optimum health benefits. Only if you are a professional runner should you have to run 5–6 times a week. 'Your warm up should include stretches' – in order to stretch safely, your muscles should be warm already. Doing stretches *after* your run will benefit you the most; a 5-minute brisk walk will help you warm up safely instead.

THERE IS SOMETHING

MAGICAL ABOUT RUNNING.

KRISTIN ARMSTRONG

Training in the company of others is often the most rewarding.

The five S's of sports
training
are: stamina, speed,
strength,
skill and spirit; but
the greatest of these is
spirit.

KEN DOHERTY

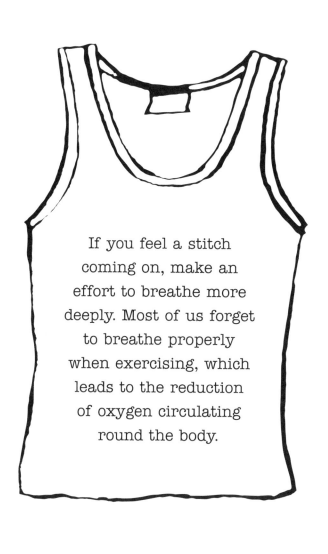

If you feel a stitch coming on, make an effort to breathe more deeply. Most of us forget to breathe properly when exercising, which leads to the reduction of oxygen circulating round the body.

DON'T DREAM OF WINNING.

TRAIN FOR IT.

MO FARAH

Start streaking – but not in the literal sense! Run Streak is a running event in America that challenges you to run at least 1 mile every day for a set amount of time – whether that's a week, a month or a year. Run Streak organise special events that often take place between two public holidays such as Memorial Day and Independence Day, or Thanksgiving and New Year.

THE MIRACLE ISN'T THAT

I FINISHED. THE MIRACLE IS THAT

I HAD THE COURAGE TO START.

JOHN BINGHAM

You've come a long way; now go that extra bit further.

I simply
love
to run. It's
almost like
the faster I go, the
easier
it becomes.

MARY DECKER

If there's a race in your local area that you haven't entered or couldn't get a place in, attend as a spectator instead and show your support for the runners. Encouraging others and being in the moment will give you the lift you need to get you itching to run.

PERSEVERANCE IS NOT A LONG RACE; IT IS MANY SHORT RACES ONE AFTER THE OTHER.

WALTER ELLIOTT

Be inspired by your running achievements by downloading a running app. There are many to choose from and some are free. Some of the most common features the free apps offer include a GPS tracker, fitness challenges and workout history, while paid-for apps include more technical add-ons, such as heart-rate zones and training analysis.

IT IS A ROUGH ROAD

THAT LEADS TO THE

HEIGHTS OF GREATNESS.

SENECA THE YOUNGER

You are the master of your achievements.

Do a little more
each day
than you think you
possibly can.

LOWELL THOMAS

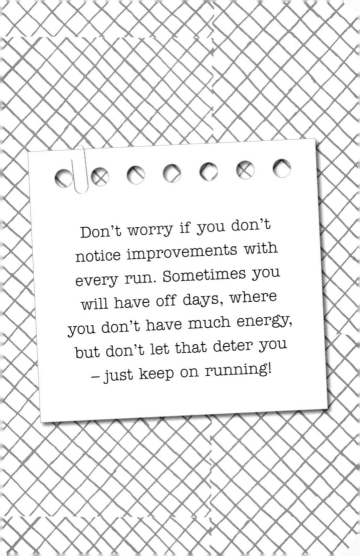

Don't worry if you don't notice improvements with every run. Sometimes you will have off days, where you don't have much energy, but don't let that deter you – just keep on running!

VISION WITHOUT ACTION

IS A DAYDREAM.

JAPANESE PROVERB

If you're working towards a goal, whether it's to run further or to run the same distance in a shorter time, be strict but realistic. Setting future goals with respective dates could help boost your motivation, as your anticipated progress is mapped out in front of you. If you have a tendency to get distracted, you might benefit from jotting down your goals to help them seem more concrete.

OUT ON THE ROADS...
THERE IS FITNESS AND SELF-
DISCOVERY AND THE PERSONS
WE WERE DESTINED TO BE.

GEORGE SHEEHAN

Run with your heart, not your mind.

There's only one **sensible** place for a person to be at 5.30 in the morning. That's in bed. I'm out running.

DEREK CLAYTON

Studies show that buying yourself a little running treat can help boost your motivation levels. Whether it's an item of clothing or a gadget, you could find that it makes you run faster and longer.

THE MOST IMPORTANT
DAY IN ANY RUNNING
PROGRAM IS REST.

HAL HIGDON

If you have a busy schedule and find it difficult to make time to go for a run, try running during your lunch break. Or, if you don't have to travel far to work, you might want to swap your car for your trainers and use the work showers to freshen up before you start the day. The feel-good hormones your body releases could help you feel less stressed and make you more productive.

I RUN BECAUSE I USED TO
BE ENVIOUS OF PEOPLE
THAT COULD RUN, AND
NOW I AM THAT PERSON.

KENDRA THOMPSON

Feel the breeze on your face; feel free.

When you're

angry,

a run can be a
sharp slap in the

face.

When happy, a
run is your

song.

DAGNY SCOTT BARRIOS

If you don't feel like going for a run, just think back to your last great run and remember how amazing it made you feel.

EVERYTHING I KNOW ABOUT LIFE,

I LEARNED IT FROM RUNNING.

ANONYMOUS

To avoid long-term injuries, be aware of how your body feels while you run. If you can feel pain or soreness, stop running. Evidence suggests that taking three days off from running is the optimum recuperation time. If you are eager to maintain your fitness levels, you can substitute running for walking or cycling on these days. When you return to running on the fourth day, try easing yourself into it by doing only half the distance you usually do. If you feel any discomfort, turn the run into a fast-paced walk.

IT DOESN'T MATTER WHETHER
YOU COME IN FIRST... OR LAST.
YOU CAN SAY, 'I HAVE FINISHED.'

FRED LEBOW

You **don't** have to go **fast;** you just have to **go.**

Feel the **fear** and do it anyway.

SUSAN JEFFERS

Did you know?

During a 10-mile run, your feet will strike the ground 15,000 times on average.

To date, Usain Bolt is the fastest human being on record. At one point during a world-record-breaking 100-metre sprint, his foot speed was recorded at a staggering 27.79 mph (44.72 km/h).

STADIUMS ARE FOR SPECTATORS.
WE RUNNERS HAVE NATURE
AND THAT IS MUCH BETTER.

JUHA VÄÄTÄINEN

It's something every runner knows, but a lot of runners often forget to do: pace yourself. Although this is an essential part of running, there are no clear-cut rules about how you should pace yourself; it's a matter of practice, how you feel and how long you intend to run for.

RUNNING IS

MY SUNSHINE.

JOAN TWINE

There is **no** such **thing** as a **regretted** run.

If you want to
achieve
a high goal, you're
going to
have to take some
chances.

ALBERTO SALAZAR

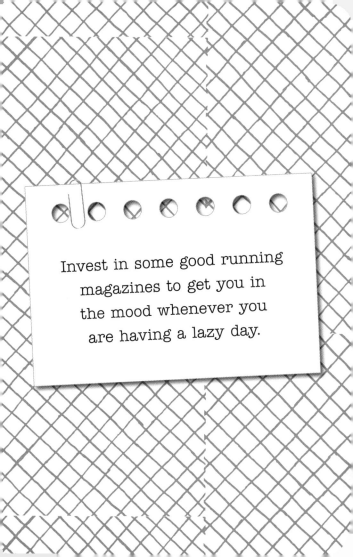

Invest in some good running
magazines to get you in
the mood whenever you
are having a lazy day.

A RUNNER MUST RUN WITH

DREAMS IN HIS HEART.

EMIL ZÁTOPEK

Many people focus on training their muscles when they run, but often forget to train their lungs. Here are some simple tips to increase lung capacity:

- It's simple, but often overlooked: concentrate on taking deep breaths to fill your lungs and help improve oxygen flow.
- Take up an additional high-intensity aerobic activity, such as swimming.
- Vary your exercise regime by doing some sprint interval training once a week.
- Try altering your training conditions to increase your levels of red blood cells. This could be running at a higher/lower altitude or in colder/warmer temperatures than usual.

THERE IS SOMETHING ABOUT THE
RITUAL OF THE RACE... THAT
BRINGS OUT THE BEST IN US.

GRETE WAITZ

Only **you** can tell yourself **when** to **stop;** there are no rules in **running.**

I run to
breathe
the fresh air.
I run to
explore.
I run to
escape
the ordinary.

DEAN KARNAZES

Keep a running money jar and every time you run, put a coin in the kitty. You'll soon have enough money to treat yourself to some new running gear. You deserve it!

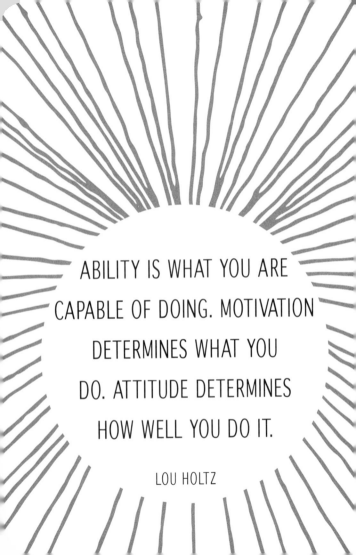

ABILITY IS WHAT YOU ARE CAPABLE OF DOING. MOTIVATION DETERMINES WHAT YOU DO. ATTITUDE DETERMINES HOW WELL YOU DO IT.

LOU HOLTZ

Don't wear cotton when you go for a run; it absorbs moisture and will leave you feeling uncomfortable. Instead choose technical fabrics, which can be bought from sports shops and specialist running shops. Technical fabrics do come at a higher price but are worth the extra expense as they help prevent chafing and skin irritation, and allow your skin to breathe.

WINNING HAS NOTHING TO DO
WITH RACING... WINNING IS
ABOUT STRUGGLE AND EFFORT
AND OPTIMISM, AND NEVER,
EVER, EVER GIVING UP.

AMBY BURFOOT

The **path** to **freedom** is just **ahead** – go **follow** it.

I don't run to
add days
to my life; I run to
add life
to my days.

ANONYMOUS

Buy a runner's
autobiography or find
a good running blog to
boost your motivation.
A professional runner's
story will give you
aspirations, while a non-
professional memoir will
give you inspiration.

I OFTEN LOSE MOTIVATION,
BUT IT'S SOMETHING I
ACCEPT AS NORMAL.

BILL RODGERS

Incorporate a fartlek (speed play) session into your running schedule; it makes training more fun and helps you build speed and endurance. Try doing 10 minutes of easy jogging, then introduce some of your own rules to combine jogging and sprinting. You could sprint in between two objects, such as lampposts, houses or benches. Then jog until you reach some traffic lights, where you begin sprinting again. The rules are yours for the making, so have fun with them!

MY MINDSET IS: IF I'M NOT
OUT THERE TRAINING,
SOMEONE ELSE IS.

LYNN JENNINGS

Training in the rain, wind and cold isn't easy, but it will make you stronger.

Every run is a
work of art,
a drawing on
each day's
canvas.

DAGNY SCOTT BARRIOS

Strengthen your core to improve your running. Try doing some abdominal exercises, such as ab twists, planks, sit-ups and donkey kicks, three times a week on top of your usual running routine.

THE BEST THING
ABOUT RUNNING IS THE
JOY IT BRINGS TO LIFE.

KARA GOUCHER

Cooling down is as essential as warming up, yet a lot of people don't do it. It allows your body to reach a resting state as efficiently as possible and helps reduce muscle tension, soreness and injury. After a run, start your cool down with a power walk and gradually slow your pace to a medium walk for 5 minutes. Then perform stretching exercises for each part of the body, holding each position for 30 seconds.

TO WIN WITHOUT RISK

IS TO TRIUMPH WITHOUT GLORY.

PIERRE CORNEILLE

Passion is pushing yourself when no one else is around.

Run hard,
be strong,
think
big!

PERCY CERUTTY

Did you know?

On average, 1 billion pairs of running trainers are sold every year worldwide. That's more than a billion people who you share the same interest with!

The first recorded Olympic running competition was in 776 BC.

TO GIVE ANYTHING LESS
THAN YOUR BEST IS TO
SACRIFICE THE GIFT.

STEVE PREFONTAINE

Always change your running shoes after a certain amount of usage – if you don't there is a higher risk of injury. The rule of thumb is to change them every 300 to 500 miles that you run; the difference between these figures is vast due to varying factors, such as how heavy your tread is and what terrain you run on. Another tell-tale sign that they need to be replaced is when you notice the top part of the sole coming away from the shoe.

SUCCESS DOESN'T COME
TO YOU; YOU GO TO IT.

MARVA COLLINS

No matter how slow you go, you are still lapping everybody on the couch.

Winning **doesn't** always mean getting **first place;** it means getting **the best** out of yourself.

MEB KEFLEZIGHI

There is an ever-growing community of runners online. Through blogs and forums you can speak to other runners about their achievements and in turn feel a part of the running community. You could even start your own running blog.

RUNNING IS ONE OF THE BEST
SOLUTIONS TO A CLEAR MIND.

SASHA AZEVEDO

If you tend to lag slightly in the last part of your run, try listening to some of these top-rated running songs to give you a boost of energy:

- 'We Are The Champions', Queen
- 'Firestarter', The Prodigy
- 'Eye of the Tiger', Survivor
- 'Born to Run', Bruce Springsteen
- '(Simply) The Best', Tina Turner
- 'Seven Nation Army', The White Stripes
- 'Take Me Out', Franz Ferdinand
- 'Are You Gonna Be My Girl', Jet

THE MORE I TRAIN,

THE MORE I REALISE I HAVE

MORE SPEED IN ME.

LEROY BURRELL

Running is
quality time
with me.

Movement
is the
essence
of life.

BERND HEINRICH

One mile of running burns approximately 100 calories. Use this mantra as an incentive to encourage you to run, and reward yourself with something healthy and tasty afterwards.

RUNNING IS ALL ABOUT

HAVING THE DESIRE TO

TRAIN AND PERSEVERE.

PAUL MAURER

To calculate your average running pace, find out how far you run and the time it takes, then divide the time by the distance. By developing a sense of pace awareness, you are more likely to set goals that are attainable. Keep checking and recording your pace every so often to track your performance.

IN ORDER TO MAKE DREAMS
COME INTO REALITY, IT
TAKES AN AWFUL LOT OF
DETERMINATION, DEDICATION,
SELF-DISCIPLINE AND EFFORT.

JESSE OWENS

A run begins with taking one small stride.

This is what **really** matters: running. This is where **I know** where I am.

STEVE JONES

If you have a dog, take it for runs instead of walks. This way you do two jobs in one!

IF YOU WANT TO BECOME
THE BEST RUNNER YOU
CAN BE, START NOW.

PRISCILLA WELCH

Many people tend to tense
up when they run, but this
actually makes it harder
to keep your movements
rhythmic. When running,
try to be aware of when
your body starts to strain
against the pressure of
your exercise. Relieve some
of the tension by relaxing
your jaw, unfurrowing your
eyebrows and bringing
your shoulders down.

THE MOST IMPORTANT MESSAGE

I STRESS TO BEGINNERS IS TO

LEARN TO LOVE THE SPORT.

CLIFF HELD

Don't wish for
it, work for it.

Running changed
my life
as it will change
yours;
just give it a
chance.

ANONYMOUS

Did you know?

Regular running is proven to help decrease chances of suffering from age-related mental illnesses. Studies show that as well as boosting your self-esteem and happiness, running is also proven to improve your memory, organisation and concentration.

THE COMPETITION IS AGAINST
THE LITTLE VOICE INSIDE YOU
THAT WANTS YOU TO QUIT.

GEORGE SHEEHAN

Running can get a little mundane when you take the same route all the time, so spice up your running scenery by trying new locations. One route could be by the coast, another in the countryside. Choosing routes that are different in terrain and incline will also add to the challenge and help you become fitter.

RUNNING MAKES
MY LIFE WHOLE.

JULIE FRONDYMAN

Whether it's a 14-minute mile or a 7-minute mile, it is still a mile.

If you have
a bad run, don't
obsess
about it. You're
always
going to have days
when your legs
feel dead.

HEATHER HANSCOM

Everybody needs a little pampering sometimes, especially runners. Book a massage as a treat when you've achieved a goal and allow yourself to be fully immersed in the calm of the moment.

GET OUT THERE AND DO
WHAT YOU LOVE!

KARA GOUCHER

To reduce your chances of getting a stitch while running, carefully choose what you eat and drink, and when you consume it. Foods that are high in fat and fibre, as well as fruit juices and sugary drinks, take longer to digest so should be avoided before a run. It is recommended that you have a low-fibre snack at least 30 minutes before you go for a run, but the longer you leave it the better.

WE MAY TRAIN OR PEAK FOR

A CERTAIN RACE, BUT RUNNING

IS A LIFETIME SPORT.

ALBERTO SALAZAR

It's **not** about being the **best.** It's about being **better** than you were **yesterday.**

Running is ultimately **a personal** experience. It is a **revival** of the spirit, a **private** oasis for the **thirsty** mind.

AMBY BURFOOT

If you're not training for a competitive race, leave your watch at home every once in a while to stop you from clock-watching.

We all have our own unique running style, but some quirks can become bad habits. Here is a list of the most common ones and how to improve them:

- Letting your hands swing across your body – your upper body has to work harder and it forces your legs to cross over each other. Instead, bend your arms from the elbow at 90° and begin the swinging momentum from the shoulders, not the forearms.

- Looking at the floor – tilting your head down reduces the oxygen supply to your body, so check yourself every so often to make sure your eyes haven't wandered to the ground.

- Landing too heavily on your feet – this can cause injury to your knees and shins. Instead, make sure your strides go steadily along the ground, but don't overstep your natural stride.

WHEN YOU RUN IN PLACES YOU
VISIT, YOU ENCOUNTER THINGS
YOU'D NEVER SEE OTHERWISE.

TOM BROKAW

On **good** days I run. On **bad** days I run **longer**.

LIFE IS COMPLICATED. RUNNING IS SIMPLE. IS IT ANY WONDER THAT PEOPLE LIKE TO RUN?

KEVIN NELSON

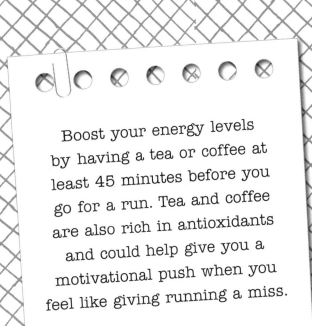

Boost your energy levels by having a tea or coffee at least 45 minutes before you go for a run. Tea and coffee are also rich in antioxidants and could help give you a motivational push when you feel like giving running a miss.

If you're interested in finding out more about our books, find us on Facebook at Summersdale Publishers and follow us on Twitter at @Summersdale.

WWW.SUMMERSDALE.COM